My name is Maria. I am a girl.
Je m'appelle Maria. Je suis une jeune fille.
Maria is ainm dom. Is cailín mé.

I am Spanish and I live in Spain.
Je suis espagnole et j'habite en Espagne
Is Spáinneach mé agus tá cónaí orm sa Spáinn.

I have dark hair and green eyes.
J'ai les cheveux noirs et les yeux verts.
Tá mo chuid gruaige dubh agus tá mo shúile glas.

I have one brother. He is a pianist. My mother is a singer.
J'ai un frère. Il est pianiste. Maman est chanteuse.
Tá deartháir amháin agam. Is pianódóir é. Amhránaí is ea mo mháthair.

I like playing tennis, riding my bike and reading books.
J'aime le tennis, le vélo et la lecture.
*Is breá liom bheith ag imirt leadóige, bheith ag rothaíocht agus
bheith ag léamh.*

bell
la sonnette
cloigín

brake
le frein
coscán

handlebars
le guidon
lámha

tyre
le pneu
bonn

D1422935

WORDBOOK
IN THREE LANGUAGES
English • French • Irish

Different types
Throughout this book the English words are printed in bold heavy type like this — **Dog**; French words are printed in ordinary type like this — le chien, and Irish words are printed in slanting type like this — *an cailín*.

How to say the words
We have not shown how the French and Irish words are pronounced. There are some sounds in both languages which are quite unlike any sound we make in English. We think it better that you should ask a teacher or any grown-up who speaks the language how to say the words in this book in the correct way.

Published in Ireland by
Gill and Macmillan Ltd
Goldenbridge
Dublin 8
with associated companies in
Auckland, Delhi, Gaborone, Hamburg,
Harare, Hong Kong, Johannesburg,
Kuala Lumpur, Lagos, London, Manzini,
Melbourne, Mexico City, Nairobi, New
York, Singapore, Tokyo

© Grisewood & Dempsey Ltd 1988
0 7171 1729 4

First published 1988 by Kingfisher Books under
the title **The Kingfisher Wordbook in Three
Languages: English, French, Spanish**

Edited by John Grisewood and Nicola Barber
Illustrated by Dave Bowyer
Handlettering by Camilla Clark
Handlettering in Irish by Peter Larrigan
Cover design: David Jefferis
Phototypeset by Southern Positives and
Negatives (SPAN), Lingfield, Surrey
Typesetting of Irish translation by
Typeworkshop Ltd, Dublin
Printed in Spain

Concept: John Grisewood
French translators: Peter Barber
Jean-Pierre Hénot
(École Primaire de Beaurainville)
Irish translator: Yvonne Carroll

CONTENTS

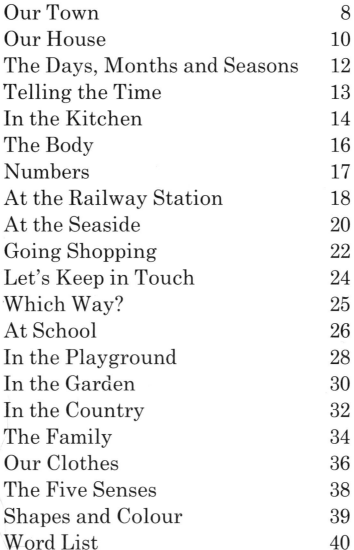

Our Town

How many people can you see in the street?

1.	**road**	la chaussée	*bóthar*
2.	**pavement**	le trottoir	*cosán*
3.	**underground station**	une station de métro	*stáisiún an fhobhealaigh*
4.	**telephone box**	une cabine téléphonique	*bosca teileafóin*
5.	**hotel**	un hôtel	*óstán*
6.	**post office**	le bureau de poste	*oifig an phoist*
7.	**litter bin**	une boite à ordures	*bosca bruscair*
8.	**chemist**	la pharmacie	*poitigéir*
9.	**policeman**	un agent de police	*garda*
10.	**baker**	une boulangerie	*báicéir*
11.	**supermarket**	un supermarché	*ollmhargadh*
12.	**offices**	les bureaux	*oifigí*
13.	**cinema**	le cinéma	*pictiúrlann*
14.	**flats**	les appartements	*árasáin*
15.	**bank**	une banque	*banc*
16.	**lamppost**	un réverbère	*cuaille lampa*
17.	**traffic lights**	les feux	*soilsí tráchta*
18.	**car**	une voiture	*carr*
19.	**parking meter**	un parcomètre	*méadar páirceála*
20.	**lorry**	un camion	*leoraí*

Our House

Do you live in a house or in a flat?

1.	**aerial**	une antenne	*aeróg*
2.	**roof**	le toit	*díon*
3.	**chimney**	la cheminée	*simléar*
4.	**attic**	le grenier	*áiléar*
5.	**bathroom**	la salle de bain	*seomra folctha*
6.	**toothbrush**	une brosse à dents	*scuab fiacal*
7.	**towel**	une serviette	*tuáille*
8.	**soap**	le savon	*gallúnach*
9.	**bed**	un lit	*leaba*
10.	**pillow**	un oreiller	*piliúr*
11.	**window**	une fenêtre	*fuinneog*
12.	**ceiling**	le plafond	*síleáil*
13.	**floor**	le plancher	*urlár*
14.	**stairs**	l'escalier	*staighre*
15.	**lamp**	une lampe	*lampa*
16.	**sitting-room**	le salon	*seomra suite*
17.	**sofa**	un canapé	*tolg*
18.	**picture**	un tableau	*pictiúr*
19.	**chair**	une chaise	*cathaoir*
20.	**kitchen**	la cuisine	*cistin*
21.	**tent**	une tente	*puball*
22.	**bone**	un os	*cnámh*
23.	**garage**	le garage	*garáiste*

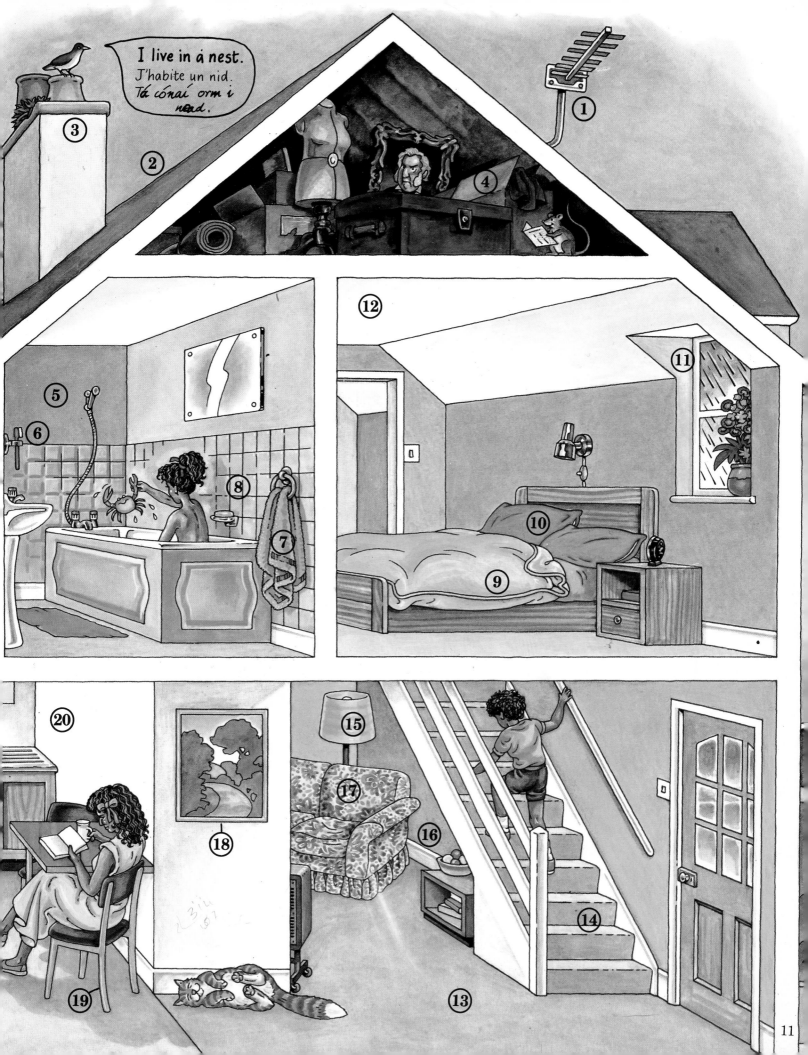

The Days, Months and Seasons

What is your favourite time of year?

THE SEASONS LES SAISONS *SÉASÚIR NA BLIANA*

Spring
Le printemps
An t-earrach

Summer
L'été
An samhradh

It's a nice day.
Il fait beau.
Lá breá atá ann.

It is warm.
Il fait chaud.
Tá sé brothallach.

Autumn
L'automne
An fómhar

Winter
L'hiver
An geimhreadh

It is windy.
Il fait du vent.
Tá sé gaofar.

It is cold.
Il fait froid.
Tá sé fuar.

1. **rain**	la pluie	*báisteach*
2. **blossom**	les fleurs des arbres	*bláth*
3. **rainbow**	un arc-en-ciel	*bogha báistí*
4. **sun**	le soleil	*grian*
5. **cloud**	un nuage	*scamall*
6. **wind**	le vent	*gaoth*
7. **leaves falling**	les feuilles qui tombent	*duilleoga ag titim*
8. **snow**	la neige	*sneachta*
9. **snowman**	un bonhomme de neige	*fear sneachta*

THE MONTHS	LES MOIS	*MÍONNA NA BLIANA*	**DAYS OF THE WEEK**	LES JOURS DE LA SEMAINE	*LAETHANTA NA SEACHTAINE*
January	janvier	*Eanáir*	**Monday**	lundi	*Luan*
February	février	*Feabhra*	**Tuesday**	mardi	*Máirt*
March	mars	*Márta*	**Wednesday**	mercredi	*Céadaoin*
April	avril	*Aibreán*	**Thursday**	jeudi	*Déardaoin*
May	mai	*Bealtaine*	**Friday**	vendredi	*Aoine*
June	juin	*Meitheamh*	**Saturday**	samedi	*Satharn*
July	juillet	*Iúil*	**Sunday**	dimanche	*Domhnach*
August	août	*Lúnasa*			
September	septembre	*Meán Fómhair*			
October	octobre	*Deireadh Fómhair*			
November	novembre	*Samhain*			
December	décembre	*Nollaig*			

Telling the Time

What's the time?
Quelle heure est-il?
Cén t-am é?

It's seven o'clock. Time to get up.
Il est sept heures. C'est l'heure de me lever.
Tá sé a seacht a chlog. Tá sé in am éirí.

yesterday
hier
inné

morning
le matin
maidin

alarm clock
un réveil
clog aláraim

It's eight-thirty. Time for school.
Il est huit heures et demie. L'heure de l'école.
Tá sé leathuair tar éis a hocht. Tá sé in am dul ar scoil.

It is twelve midday. Lunch time.
Il est midi. L'heure du déjeuner.
Tá sé ina mheán lae. Am lóin.

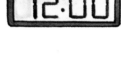

afternoon
l'après-midi
tráthnóna

wrist watch
une montre
uaireadóir

today
aujourd'hui
inniu

It's a quarter to eight. Story time.
Il est huit heures moins le quart. L'heure de raconter une histoire.
Tá sé ceathrú chun a hocht. Am scéalta.

evening
le soir
iarnóin

It's a quarter past eight. Bedtime.
Il est huit heures et quart. L'heure d'aller au lit.
Tá sé ceathrú tar éis a hocht. Am codlata.

clock
une pendule
clog

It is midnight. It is dark outside.
Il est minuit. Dehors, il fait noir.
Tá sé ina mheán oíche. Tá sé dorcha lasmuigh.

night
la nuit
oíche

tomorrow
demain
amárach

13

In the Kitchen

We nearly always eat in the kitchen.

1.	**sink**	l'évier	*doirteal*
2.	**tap**	un robinet	*sconna*
3.	**can-opener**	un ouvre-boîtes	*osclóir*
4.	**vegetable rack**	un casier à légumes	*raca glasraí*
5.	**electric-mixer**	un batteur éléctrique	*meascthóir leictreach*
6.	**washing machine**	une machine à laver	*meaisín níocháin*
7.	**dishwasher**	un lave-vaisselle	*miasniteoir*
8.	**rolling-pin**	un rouleau	*crann fuinte*
9.	**dustbin**	une poubelle	*bosca bruscair*
10.	**fridge**	un réfrigérateur	*cuisneoir*
11.	**broom**	un balai	*scuab*
12.	**saucepan**	une casserole	*sáspan*
13.	**frying-pan**	une poêle	*friochtán*
14.	**cooker**	une cuisinière	*sorn*
15.	**table**	une table	*bord*
16.	**stool**	un tabouret	*stól*
17.	**coffee pot**	une cafetière	*caifephota*
18.	**bowl**	un bol	*babhla*
19.	**jug**	un pot	*crúiscín*
20.	**iron**	un fer	*iarann*
21.	**ironing-board**	une planche à repasser	*bord iarnála*
22.	**cup and saucer**	une tasse et une soucoupe	*cupán agus sásar*

kettle
une bouilloire
citeal

corkscrew
un tire-bouchon
corcscriú

spoon
une cuillère
spúnóg

knife
un couteau
scian

plate
une assiette
pláta

I am hungry. What are you eating?
J'ai faim. Qu'est-ce que tu manges?
Tá ocras orm. Céard atá á ithe agaibh?

We are eating bananas and cake.
Nous mangeons les bananes, et un gâteau.
Táimid ag ithe bananaí agus cáca.

Dad is in the kitchen cooking breakfast.
Papa est dans la cuisine. Il prépare le petit déjeuner.
Tá Daidí sa chistin ag ullmhú an bhricfeasta.

The Body
From Head to Toe.

foot le pied *cos*

back le dos *droim*

face la figure *aghaidh*

shoulder l'épaule *gualainn*

leg la jambe *troigh*

stomach l'estomac *bolg*

chest la poitrine *cliabh*

arm le bras *géag*

hand la main *lámh*

Come on in! The water is lovely!
Viens! L'eau est bonne!
Tar isteach! Tá an t-uisce go hálainn!

head la tête

1.	**mouth**	la bouche	*béal*
2.	**nose**	le nez	*srón*
3.	**eye (eyes)**	l'oeil (les yeux)	*súil*
4.	**ear**	l'oreille	*cluas*
5.	**hair**	les cheveux	*gruaig*
6.	**neck**	le cou	*muineál*
7.	**elbow**	le coude	*uillinn*
8.	**finger**	le doigt	*méar*
9.	**thumb**	le pouce	*ordóg*
10.	**knee**	le genou	*glúin*
11.	**ankle**	la cheville	*murnán*
12.	**toe**	l'orteil	*barraicín*

Numbers

Can you count up to 20?

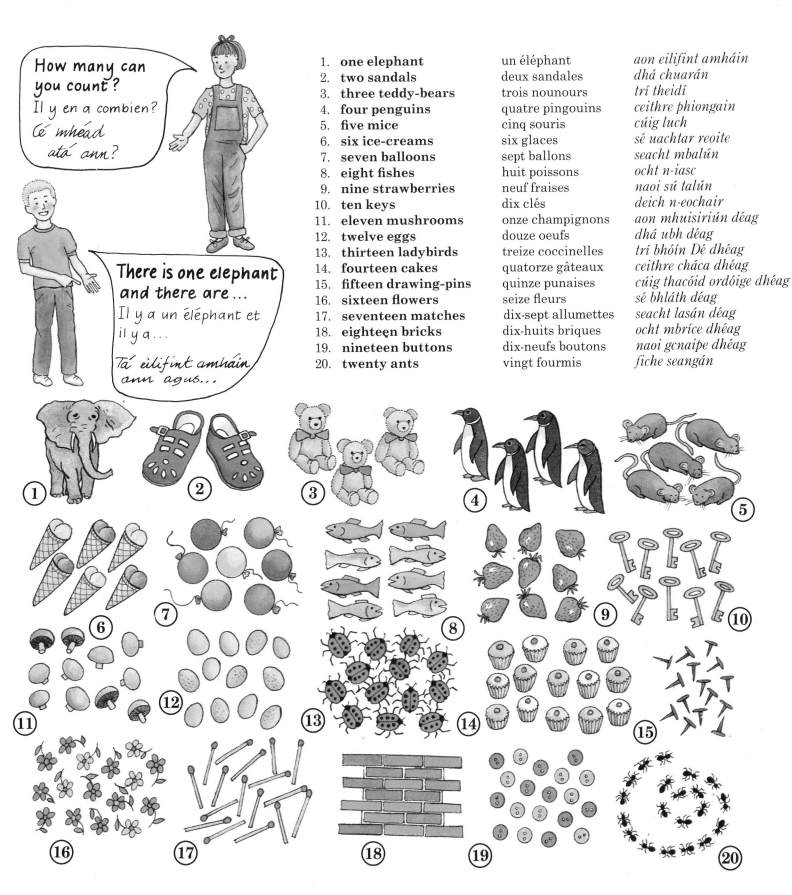

How many can you count?

Il y en a combien?

Cé mhéad atá ann?

There is one elephant and there are...

Il y a un éléphant et il y a...

Tá eilifint amháin ann agus...

1.	one elephant	un éléphant	*aon eilifint amháin*
2.	two sandals	deux sandales	*dhá chuarán*
3.	three teddy-bears	trois nounours	*trí theidí*
4.	four penguins	quatre pingouins	*ceithre phiongain*
5.	five mice	cinq souris	*cúig luch*
6.	six ice-creams	six glaces	*sé uachtar reoite*
7.	seven balloons	sept ballons	*seacht mbalún*
8.	eight fishes	huit poissons	*ocht n-iasc*
9.	nine strawberries	neuf fraises	*naoi sú talún*
10.	ten keys	dix clés	*deich n-eochair*
11.	eleven mushrooms	onze champignons	*aon mhuisiriún déag*
12.	twelve eggs	douze oeufs	*dhá ubh déag*
13.	thirteen ladybirds	treize coccinelles	*trí bhóín Dé dhéag*
14.	fourteen cakes	quatorze gâteaux	*ceithre cháca dhéag*
15.	fifteen drawing-pins	quinze punaises	*cúig thacóid ordóige dhéag*
16.	sixteen flowers	seize fleurs	*sé bhláth déag*
17.	seventeen matches	dix-sept allumettes	*seacht lasán déag*
18.	eighteen bricks	dix-huits briques	*ocht mbríce dhéag*
19.	nineteen buttons	dix-neufs boutons	*naoi gcnaipe dhéag*
20.	twenty ants	vingt fourmis	*fiche seangán*

At the Railway Station

Here we are at the station. Hurry up or we'll miss the train!

1.	**train**	un train	*traein*
2.	**engine-driver**	le conducteur	*tiománaí traenach*
3.	**locomotive**	une locomotive	*inneall*
4.	**railway line**	la voie ferrée	*bóthar iarainn*
5.	**platform**	le quai	*ardán*
6.	**carriage**	un wagon	*carráiste*
7.	**guard**	le chef de train	*garda*
8.	**flag**	un drapeau	*bratach*
9.	**porter**	un porteur	*póirtéir*
10.	**luggage trolley**	un chariot à bagages	*tralaí*
11.	**luggage**	les bagages	*bagáiste*
12.	**passenger**	un voyageur/ une voyageuse	*paisinéir*
13.	**signal**	un signal	*comhartha*
14.	**exit**	la sortie	*bealach amach*
15.	**subway**	un souterrain	*fobhealach*
16.	**newspaper**	un journal	*nuachtán*
17.	**newsagent**	un marchand de journaux	*nuachtánaí*
18.	**handbag**	un sac à main	*mála láimhe*
19.	**platform number**	le numéro du quai	*uimhir ardáin*
20.	**refreshment kiosk**	un buffet	*siopa bia*

At the Seaside

In summer it is fun to go to the beach all day.

1.	**sky**	le ciel	*spéir*
2.	**sun**	le soleil	*grian*
3.	**cloud**	un nuage	*scamall*
4.	**sand**	le sable	*gaineamh*
5.	**sea**	la mer	*farraige*
6.	**wave**	une vague	*tonn*
7.	**cliff**	une falaise	*aill*
8.	**cave**	une caverne	*pluais*
9.	**seagull**	une mouette	*faoileán*
10.	**yacht**	un voilier	*luamh*
11.	**sail**	une voile	*seol*
12.	**mast**	un mât	*crann seoil*
13.	**rowing-boat**	un bateau à rames	*bád rámhaíochta*
14.	**motor boat**	une vedette	*bád mótair*
15.	**fish**	un poisson	*iasc*
16.	**surfer**	un surfeur	*marcach toinne*
17.	**rock**	un rocher	*carraig*
18.	**seaweed**	le varech	*feamainn*
19.	**ship**	un navire	*long*
20.	**bucket**	un seau	*buicéad*
21.	**spade·**	une pelle	*spád*
22.	**raft**	un radeau	*rafta*
23.	**umbrella**	un parasol	*scáth gréine*
24.	**deck-chair**	un transatlantique	*cathaoir deice*
25.	**lighthouse**	un phare	*teach solais*

20

Going Shopping

We buy our food at the supermarket. We often meet our friends there.

	English	French	Irish
1.	fruit	les fruits	torthaí
2.	vegetables	les légumes	glasraí
3.	meat	la viande	feoil
4.	fish	le poisson	iasc
5.	bread	le pain	arán
6.	cake	le gâteau	cáca
7.	sugar	le sucre	siúcra
8.	milk	le lait	bainne
9.	eggs	les oeufs	uibheacha
10.	cheese	le fromage	cáis
11.	butter	le beurre	im
12.	pears	les poires	piorraí
13.	apples	les pommes	úlla
14.	bananas	les bananes	bananaí
15.	potatoes	les pommes de terre	prátaí
16.	onions	les oignons	oinniúin
17.	carrots	les carottes	cairéid
18.	cauliflower	un chou-fleur	cóilís
19.	wine	le vin	fíon
20.	check-out	la caisse	deasc airgid
21.	trolley	un chariot	tralaí
22.	cashier	la caissière	airgeadóir
23.	money	l'argent	airgead

strawberry
une fraise
sú talún

raspberry
une framboise
sú chraobh

lemon
un citron
líomóid

mushroom
un champignon
muisiriún

23

Let's keep in touch

1. **newspaper**   un journal   *nuachtán*
2. **books**   les livres   *leabhair*
3. **television**   un téléviseur   *teilifíseán*
4. **radio**   la radio   *raidió*
5. **typewriter**   une machine à écrire   *clóscríobhán*
6. **letter**   une lettre   *litir*
7. **envelope**   une enveloppe   *clúdach litreach*
8. **stamp**   un timbre-poste   *stampa*
9. **address**   une adresse   *seoladh*
10. **pen**   un stylo   *peann*
11. **photograph**   une photographie   *grianghraf*
12. **telephone**   un téléphone   *teileafón*
13. **camera**   un appareil   *ceamara*
14. **calculator**   une calculatrice   *áireamhán*

Which Way?

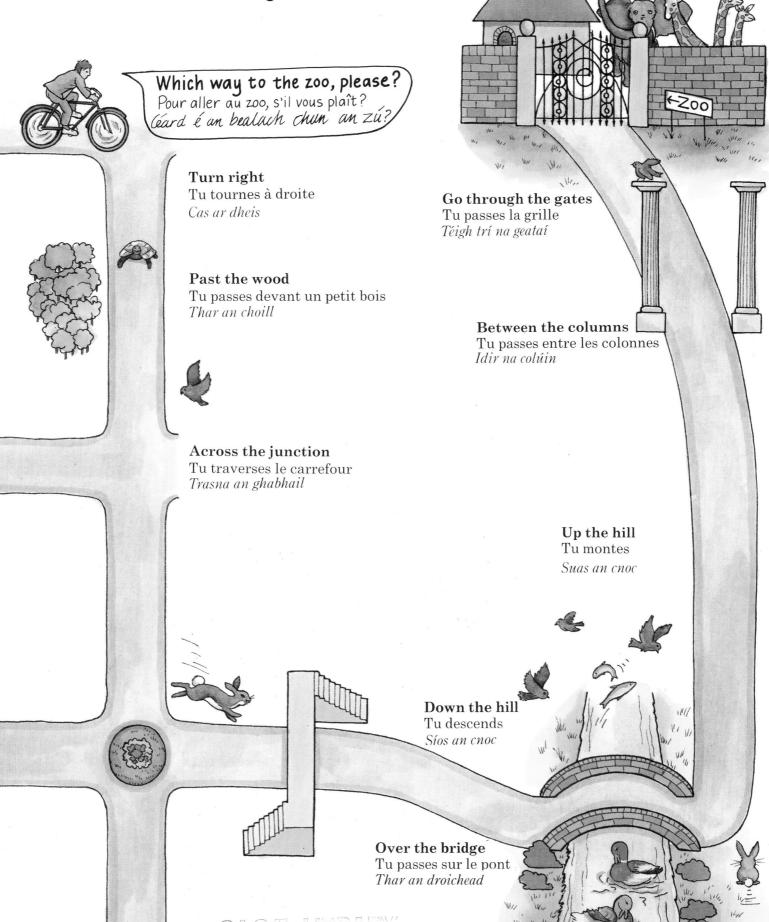

Which way to the zoo, please?
Pour aller au zoo, s'il vous plaît?
Céard é an bealach chun an zú?

Turn right
Tu tournes à droite
Cas ar dheis

Past the wood
Tu passes devant un petit bois
Thar an choill

Across the junction
Tu traverses le carrefour
Trasna an ghabhail

Go through the gates
Tu passes la grille
Téigh trí na geataí

Between the columns
Tu passes entre les colonnes
Idir na colúin

Up the hill
Tu montes
Suas an cnoc

Down the hill
Tu descends
Síos an cnoc

Over the bridge
Tu passes sur le pont
Thar an droichead

←ZOO

At School

School is fun. There are so many things to learn and do.

1.	**blackboard**	un tableau noir	*clár dubh*
2.	**globe**	un globe terrestre	*cruinneog*
3.	**easel**	un chevalet	*tacas*
4.	**abacus**	un abaque	*fráma comhairimh*
5.	**teacher**	une institutrice	*múinteoir*
6.	**pupil (boy)**	un écolier	*dalta (buachaill)*
	pupil (girl)	une écolière	*dalta (cailín)*
7.	**paints**	les couleurs	*péinteanna*
8.	**paintbrushes**	les pinceaux	*scuabanna péinteála*
9.	**painting**	la peinture	*ag dathú*
10.	**exercise-book**	un cahier	*cóipleabhar*
11.	**paper**	le papier	*páipéar*
12.	**alphabet**	l'alphabet	*aibítir*
13.	**sums**	les calculs	*suimeanna*
14.	**satchel**	un cartable	*mála scoile*
15.	**wastepaper-basket**	une corbeille à papier	*ciseán bruscair*
16.	**cupboard**	une armoire	*cófra*
17.	**chalk**	la craie	*cailc*
18.	**goldfish**	un poisson rouge	*iasc órga*
19.	**books**	les livres	*leabhair*

It's easy to learn how to speak English.

Apprendre l'anglais, ce n'est pas difficile.

Is furasta an Béarla a fhoghlaim.

pencil-sharpener
un taille-crayons
bioróir

drawing-pin
une punaise
tacóid ordóige

scissors
les ciseaux
siosúr

ruler
une régle
rialóir

pencil
un crayon
peann luaidhe

In the Playground

What a lot of different things the children are doing in the playground.

1.	**walk**	marcher	*siúil*
2.	**stand**	se tenir debout	*seas*
3.	**jump**	sauter	*léim*
4.	**skip**	sauter à la corde	*scipeáil*
5.	**sit**	être assis	*suigh*
6.	**run**	courir	*rith*
7.	**throw**	lancer	*caith*
8.	**catch**	attraper	*beir*
9.	**pull**	tirer	*tarraing*
10.	**push**	pousser	*brúigh*
11.	**fall down**	tomber	*tit*
12.	**eat**	manger	*ith*
13.	**drink**	boire	*ól*
14.	**wave**	saluer	*croith (lámh)*
15.	**smile**	sourire	*déan meangadh*
16.	**cry**	pleurer	*goil*
17.	**read**	lire	*léigh*

18.	**bend**	se pencher	*lúb*	
19.	**hop**	sauter à cloche-pied	*preab*	**play**
20.	**climb**	grimper	*dreap*	jouer
21.	**give**	donner	*tabhair*	*imir*
22.	**take**	prendre	*tóg*	
23.	**speak**	parler	*labhair*	
24.	**listen**	écouter	*éist*	

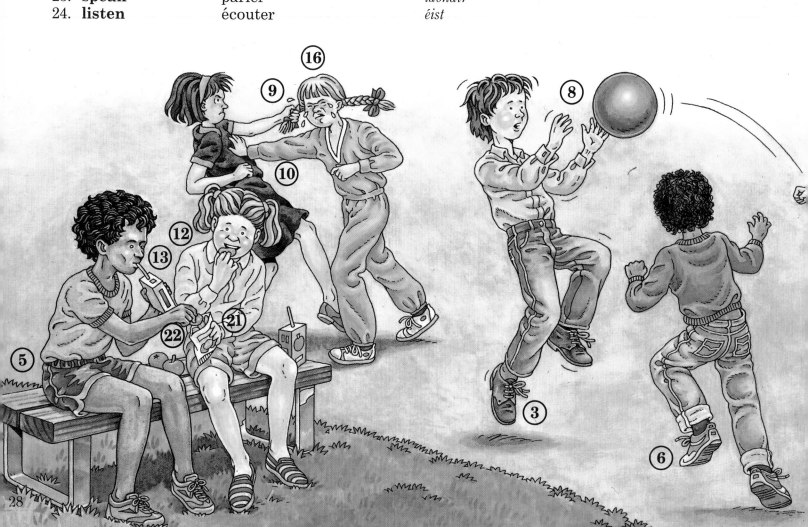

Do you speak English?
Parlez-vous anglais?
An labhraíonn tú Béarla?

No, but
Non, mais . . .
Ní labhraím, ach ...

I speak French	Je parle français	*Labhraím Fraincis*
You speak German	Tu parles allemand	*Labhraíonn tú Gearmáinis*
He speaks Spanish	Il parle espagnol.	*Labhraíonn sé Spáinnis*
She speaks Chinese	Elle parle chinois	*Labhraíonn sí Sínis*
We speak Italian	Nous parlons italien	*Labhraímid Iodáilis*
You speak Russian	Vous parlez russe	*Labhraíonn sibh Rúisis*
They speak Portuguese	Ils parlent portugais	*Labhraíonn siad Portaingéilis*
They speak Swedish	Elles parlent suédois	*Labhraíonn siad Sualainnis*

In the Garden
All kinds of plants grow in a garden.

1. **tree** — un arbre — *crann*
2. **leaf** — une feuille — *duilleog*
3. **bush** — un arbuste — *tor*
4. **grass** — le gazon — *féar*
5. **lawnmower** — une tondeuse — *lomaire faiche*
6. **flowerbed** — une plate-bande — *bláthcheapach*
7. **worm** — un ver — *péist*
8. **wheelbarrow** — une brouette — *barra rotha*
9. **watering-can** — un arrosoir — *canna spréite*
10. **greenhouse** — une serre — *teach gloine*
11. **spade** — une bêche — *spád*
12. **fork** — une fourche — *forc gairdín*
13. **swing** — une balançoire — *luascán*
14. **see-saw** — une bascule — *maide corrach*
15. **fence** — une clôture — *fál*
16. **vegetables** — les légumes — *glasraí*
17. **hosepipe** — un tuyau — *píobán uisce*
18. **earth** — la terre — *cré*
19. **pond** — un bassin — *lochán*
20. **path** — une allée — *cosán*

rose
une rose
rós

flowerpot
un pot à fleurs
próca bláthanna

trowel
une houlette
lián

In the Country

Look carefully around the countryside. You can see lots of animals

1.	**farmhouse**	une maison de ferme	*teach feirme*
2.	**farmer**	le fermier	*feirmeoir*
3.	**chicken**	les poulets	*sicín*
4.	**pig**	un cochon	*muc*
5.	**cow**	une vache	*bó*
6.	**calf**	un veau	*lao*
7.	**sheep**	un mouton	*caora*
8.	**lamb**	un agneau	*uan*
9.	**hill**	une colline	*cnoc*
10.	**mountain**	une montagne	*sliabh*
11.	**village**	un village	*sráidbhaile*
12.	**wood**	un bois	*coill*
13.	**horse**	un cheval	*capall*
14.	**tractor**	un tracteur	*tarracóir*
15.	**plough**	une charrue	*céachta*
16.	**turkey**	un dindon	*turcaí*
17.	**fox**	un renard	*sionnach*
18.	**hedge**	une haie	*fál*
19.	**rabbit**	un lapin	*coinín*
20.	**squirrel**	un écureuil	*iora rua*

cheese
le fromage
cáis

milk
le lait
bainne

butter
la beurre
im

The Family

The whole family is arriving to wish Gran a happy birthday.

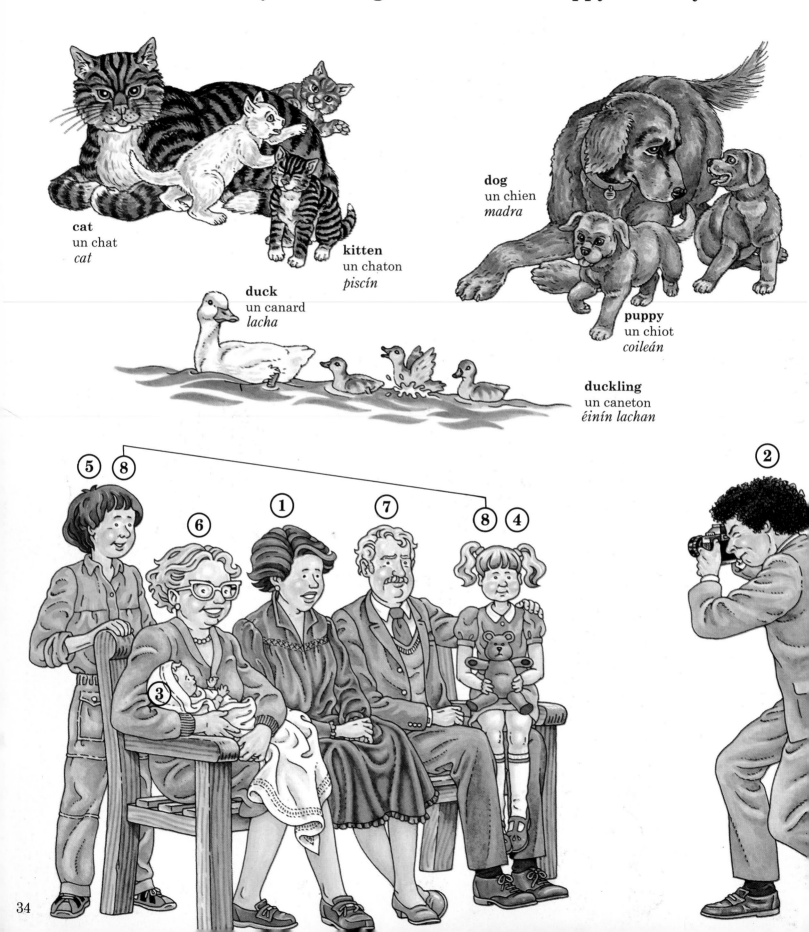

cat
un chat
cat

kitten
un chaton
piscín

dog
un chien
madra

puppy
un chiot
coileán

duck
un canard
lacha

duckling
un caneton
éinín lachan

1. **mother (mummy)**	la mère (maman)	*máthair (mamaí)*
2. **father (daddy)**	le père (papa)	*athair (daidí)*
3. **baby**	le bébé	*leanbh*
4. **daughter**	la fille	*iníon*
5. **son**	le fils	*mac*
6. **grandmother/wife**	la grand-mère/la femme	*mamó/bean chéile*
7. **grandfather/husband**	le grand-père/le mari	*daideo/fear céile*
8. **grandchildren**	les petits-enfants	*clann clainne*
9. **uncle**	l'oncle	*uncail*
10. **aunt**	la tante	*aintín*
11. **cousin**	le cousin (boy) la cousine (girl)	*col ceathar*
12. **brother**	le frère	*deartháir*
13. **sister**	la soeur	*deirfiúr*
14. **nephew**	le neveu	*nia*
15. **niece**	la nièce	*neacht*
16. **present**	un cadeau	*bronntanas*
17. **flowers**	les fleurs	*bláthanna*

This is my brother. I am his sister. We belong to the same family.

Voici mon frère. Je suis sa soeur. Nous sommes de la même famille.

Seo é mo dheartháir. Is mise a dheirfiúr. Is den chlann chéanna muid.

Our Clothes
It is cold today. What can we wear?

1.	**dress**	une robe	*gúna*
2.	**skirt**	une jupe	*sciorta*
3.	**jeans**	un jean	*brístí géine*
4.	**socks**	les chaussettes	*stocaí*
5.	**shoes**	les chaussures	*bróga*
6.	**gloves**	les gants	*lámhainní*
7.	**hat**	un chapeau	*hata*
8.	**sweater**	un chandail	*geansaí*
9.	**belt**	une ceinture	*crios*
10.	**jacket**	un veston	*seaicéad*
11.	**trousers**	un pantalon	*brístí*
12.	**underpants**	un slip	*brístíní*
13.	**vest**	un maillot de corps	*veist*
14.	**shirt**	une chemise	*léine*
15.	**tie**	une cravate	*carbhat*
16.	**pyjamas**	un pyjama	*culaith leapa*
17.	**dressing-gown**	une robe de chambre	*fallaing sheomra*
18.	**slippers**	les pantoufles	*slipéirí*
19.	**raincoat**	un imperméable	*cóta báistí*
20.	**overcoat**	un pardessus	*cóta mór*
21.	**wardrobe**	une garde-robe	*vardrús*
22.	**mirror**	une glace/un miroir	*scáthán*
23.	**hanger**	un cintre	*crochadán*

36

handkerchief
un mouchoir
ciarsúr

comb
un peigne
cíor

hairbrush
une brosse à cheveux
scuab gruaige

The things we wear are called clothes.
Ce que nous portons, ce sont des vêtements.
Glaoimid éadaí ar na nithe a chaithimid.

Most clothes are made of cloth.
La plupart des vêtements sont en étoffe de laine.
Déantar formhór ár gcuid éadaí as éadach.

The Five Senses

sight
la vue
radharc

Look at the balloon in the sky. Can you see it?
Regarde le ballon dans le ciel. Tu peux le voir?
Féach ar an mbalún sa spéir. An féidir leat é a fheiceáil?

hearing
l'ouïe
éisteacht

Listen to the lion roaring. Can you hear him?
Écoute le lion qui rugit. Tu peux l'entendre?
Éist leis an leon ag búiríl. An féidir leat é a chloisteáil?

smell
l'odorat
boladh

Smell the flowers. Can you smell the scent?
Sens les fleurs. Tu peux en sentir l'odeur?
Bolaigh na bláthanna. An féidir leat an chumhracht a bholadh?

Taste the ice-cream. Can you taste the chocolate?
Goûte la glace. Tu peux en sentir le parfum de chocolat?
Blais an t-uachtar reoite. An féidir leat an tseacláid a bhlaiseadh?

taste
le goût
blas

Touch the cat's fur. Can you feel how soft it is?
Touche la fourrure du chat. Tu peux sentir comme elle est douce?
Cuimil fionnadh an chait. Féach chomh bog is atá sé.

touch
le toucher
tadhall

Touch the table. Can you feel how hard it is?
Touche la table. Tu peux sentir comme elle est dure?
Leag do lámh ar an mbord. Féach chomh crua is atá sé.

Shapes and Colours

When you mix colours together you make new colours.

a pink rectangle
un rectangle rose
dronuilleog bhándearg

a red circle
un cercle rouge
ciorcal dearg

a black oval
un ovale noir
ubhchruth dubh

a white square
un carré blanc
cearnóg bhán

a yellow star
une étoile jaune
réalta bhuí

a blue sphere
une sphère bleue
sféar gorm

a purple heart
un coeur violet
croí corcra

a brown cube
un cube brun
ciúb donn

an orange pyramid
une pyramide orange
pirimid oráiste

Blue and yellow make green.
Le bleu et le jaune produisent le vert
Tugann gorm agus buí uaine mar thoradh.

WORD LIST

bird
un oiseau
éan

ENGLISH	FRENCH	IRISH
abacus	un abaque	*fráma comhairimh*
address	une adresse	*seoladh*
aerial	une antenne	*aeróg*
aeroplane	un avion	*eitleán*
afternoon	un après-midi	*iarnóin*
airport	un aéroport	*aerphort*
alarm clock	un réveil	*clog aláraim*
alphabet	un alphabet	*aibítir*
ankle	la cheville	*murnán*
ant	un fourmi	*seangán*
apple	une pomme	*úll*
April	avril	*Aibreán*
arm	le bras	*géag*
attic	un grenier	*áiléar*
August	août	*Lúnasa*
aunt	une tante	*aintín*
autumn	automne	*an fómhar*
baby	un bébé	*leanbh*
baker's (shop)	une boulangerie	*siopa an bháicéara*
balloon	un ballon	*balún*
banana	une banane	*banana*
bank	une banque	*banc*
to bark	aboyer	*tafann*
bathroom	une salle de bain	*seomra folctha*
bed	un lit	*leaba*
bell (small, hand-)	une sonnette	*cloigín*
belt	une ceinture	*crios*
to bend	se pencher	*crom*
between	entre	*idir*
bicycle	un vélo	*rothar*
bird	un oiseau	*éan*
black	noir, noire	*dubh*
blackboard	un tableau noir	*clár dubh*
blossom	les fleurs des arbres	*bláth*
blue	bleu, bleue	*gorm*
body	le corps	*corp*
bone	un os	*cnámh*
book	un livre	*leabhar*
bowl	un bol	*babhla*
boy	un garçon	*buachaill*
brake	un frein	*coscán*
bread	le pain	*arán*
breakfast	le petit déjeuner	*bricfeasta*
brick	une brique	*bríce*
bridge	un pont	*droichead*
broom	un balai	*scuab*
brother	un frère	*deartháir*
brown	brun, brune	*donn*
bucket	un seau	*buicéad*
to build	construire, faire	*tóg*
bush	un arbuste	*tor*
but	mais	*ach*
butter	le beurre	*im*
button	un bouton	*cnaipe*
to buy	acheter	*ceannaigh*
cake	un gâteau	*cáca*
calculator	une calculatrice	*áireamhán*
calendar	un calendrier	*féilire*
calf	un veau	*lao*
camera	un appareil (photographique)	*ceamara*
can (= to be able to, know how to)	savoir	*is féidir le*
can-opener	un ouvre-boîtes	*osclóir*
car	une automobile, une voiture	*carr*

carriage	le wagon	*carráiste*
carrot	une carotte	*cairéad*
cashier	une caissière	*airgeadóir*
cat	un chat	*cat*
to catch	attraper	*beir ar*
cauliflower	un chou-fleur	*cóilís*
cave	une caverne	*pluais*
ceiling	un plafond	*síleáil*
chair	une chaise	*cathaoir*
chalk	la craie	*cailc*
check-out (supermarket)	une caisse	*deasc airgid*
cheese	un fromage	*cáis*
chemist's (shop)	une pharmacie	*siopa an phoitigéara*
chest (part of body)	la poitrine	*cliabh*
chicken	un poulet	*sicín*
child	un enfant	*páiste*
chimney	une cheminée	*simléar*
cinema	un cinéma	*pictiúrlann*
circle	un cercle	*ciorcal*
classroom	une salle de classe	*seomra ranga*
cliff	une falaise	*aill*
to climb	grimper	*dreap*
clock (household)	une pendule	*clog*
cloth	une étoffe	*éadach*
clothes	les vêtements	*éadaí*
cloud	un nuage	*scamall*
coffee pot	une cafetière	*caifephota*
cold	froid, froide	*fuar*
colour	une couleur	*dath*
comb	un peigne	*cíor*
control tower (airport)	une tour de contrôle	*túr stiúrtha*
cooker	une cuisinière	*sorn*

aeroplane
un avion
eitleán

balloon
un ballon
balún

control tower
une tour de contrôle
túr stiúrtha

corkscrew	un tire-bouchon	*corcscriú*
corner	un coin	*cúinne*
to count	compter	*comhaireamh*
cousin	un cousin, une cousine	*col ceathar*
cow	une vache	*bó*
crab	un crabe	*portán*
to cry	pleurer	*goil*
cube	un cube	*ciúb*
cup	une tasse	*cupán*
cupboard	une armoire	*cófra*
dad, daddy	papa	*daidí*
(it is) dark	il fait noir	*tá sé dorcha*
date	la date	*dáta*
daughter	une fille	*iníon*
day	un jour	*lá*
December	décembre	*Nollaig*
deck-chair	un transatlantique	*cathaoir deice*
to dig	bêcher	*rómhar*
dishwasher	un lave-vaisselle	*miasniteoir*
to dive	plonger	*tumadh*
to do	faire	*déan*
dog	un chien	*madra*
door	une porte	*doras*
to draw	dessiner	*tarraing*
drawer	un tiroir	*tarraiceán*
drawing-pin	une punaise	*tacóid ordóige*
dress	une robe	*gúna*
dressing-gown	un peignoir	*fallaing sheomra*
to drink	boire	*ól*
duck	un canard	*lacha*
dustbin	une poubelle	*bosca bruscair*
ear	une oreille	*cluas*
earth	la terre	*cré*
easel	un chevalet	*tacas*
to eat	manger	*ith*
egg	un oeuf	*ubh*
eight	huit	*a hocht*
eighteen	dix-huit	*a hocht déag*
elbow	le coude	*uillinn*
electric-mixer	un batteur électrique	*meascthóir leictreach*
elephant	un éléphant	*eilifint*
eleven	onze	*a haon déag*
envelope	une enveloppe	*clúdach litreach*
evening	un soir	*oíche*
exercise-book	un cahier	*cóipleabhar*
exit	la sortie	*bealach amach*
eye, eyes	l'oeil, les yeux	*súil, súile*
face	la figure, le visage	*aghaidh*
to fall	tomber	*tit*
family	une famille	*clann*
farm/farmhouse	une ferme/une maison de ferme	*feirm/teach feirme*
farmer	un fermier	*feirmeoir*
father	le père	*athair*
February	février	*Feabhra*
fence	une clôture	*fál*
fifteen	quinze	*a cúig déag*
finger	le doigt	*méar*
fish	un poisson	*iasc*
five	cinq	*a cúig*
flag	un drapeau	*bratach*
flats	les appartements	*árasáin*
floor	un plancher	*urlár*
flower	une fleur	*bláth*
flowerbed	une plate-bande	*bláthcheapach*
flowerpot	un pot à fleurs	*próca bláthanna*

glider
un planeur
faoileoir

foot	le pied	*troigh*
fork (garden)	une fourche	*forc gairdín*
fork (table)	une fourchette	*forc*
four	quatre	*a ceathair*
fourteen	quatorze	*a ceathair déag*
fox	un renard	*sionnach*
Friday	vendredi	*Aoine*
fridge	un réfrigérateur, un frigo	*cuisneoir*
friend	un ami, une amie	*cara*
fruit	un fruit	*torthaí*
frying-pan	une poêle (à frire)	*friochtán*
garden	un jardin	*gairdin*
gate	une barrière; une grille	*geata*
to give	donner	*tabhair*
glider	un planeur	*faoileoir*
globe (in classroom)	un globe terrestre	*cruinneog*
glove	un gant	*lámhainn*
to go	aller	*téigh*
goldfish	un poisson rouge	*iasc órga*
grandchildren	les petits-enfants	*clann clainne*
grandfather	un grand-père	*daideo*
grandmother/ granny	une grand-mère/grand-maman	*mamó*
grass	le gazon/l'herbe	*féar*
green	vert, verte	*uaine*
greenhouse	une serre	*teach gloine*
guard (railway)	un chef de train	*garda*
hair	les cheveux	*gruaig*
half	la moitié	*leath*
hand	la main	*lámh*
handbag	un sac à main	*mála láimhe*
handkerchief	un mouchoir	*ciarsúr*
handlebar	un guidon	*lámha*
hanger	un cintre	*crochadán*
hat	un chapeau	*hata*
to have	avoir	*tá ag …*
head	la tête	*ceann*
to hear	entendre	*clois*
heart	le coeur	*croí*
hedge	une haie	*claí*
helicopter	un hélicoptère	*héileacaptar*
hill	une colline	*cnoc*
to hop	sauter à cloche-pied	*preab*
horse	un cheval	*capall*
hosepipe	un tuyau	*píobán uisce*
hot	chaud, chaude	*te*
hotel	un hôtel	*óstán*
hour	une heure	*uair*
house	une maison	*teach*
hungry/I'm hungry	faim/j'ai faim	*ocrach/tá ocras orm*
husband	un mari	*fear céile*

helicopter
un hélicoptère
héileacaptar

I/I'm a boy	je/je suis un garçon	mé/is buachaill mé
ice	la glace	oighear
ice cream	une glace	uachtar reoite
iron	un fer à repasser	iarann
ironing-board	une planche à repasser	bord iarnála
it's	c'est	is/tá
jacket	un veston	seaicéad
January	janvier	Eanáir
jeans	un jean, un blue-jean	brístí géine
jet-engine	un moteur à réaction	scairdinneall
jug	un pot	crúiscín
July	juillet	Iúil
to jump	sauter	léim
June	juin	Meitheamh
kennel	une niche	cró
kettle	une bouilloire	citeal
key	une clé, une clef	eochair
kitchen	une cuisine	cistin
kite	un cerf-volant	eitleog
kitten	un chaton	piscín
knee	le genou	glúin
knife	un couteau	scian
ladybird	un coccinelle	bóín Dé
lamb	un agneau	uan
lamp	une lampe	lampa
lamppost	un réverbère	cuaille lampa
lawnmower	une tondeuse	lomaire faiche
leaf	une feuille	duilleog
to learn	apprendre	foghlaim
to leave	partir, quitter	fág
left	la gauche	ar clé
leg	la jambe	cos
lemon	un citron	líomóid
letter	une lettre	litir
lighthouse	un phare	teach solais
lion	le lion	leon
to listen	écouter	éist
litter bin	une boite à ordures	bosca bruscair
living-room	une salle de séjour	seomra teaghlaigh
to look	regarder	féach
lorry	un camion, un poids lourd	leoraí
luggage	les bagages	bagáiste
to make	faire	déan
man	un homme	fear
March	mars	Márta
mast	un mât	crann seoil
match	une allumette	lasán
May	mai	Bealtaine
meat	la viande	feoil
midday	midi	meán lae
midnight	minuit	meán oíche
milk	le lait	bainne
mirror	un miroir, une glace	scáthán
Monday	lundi	Luan
money	l'argent	airgead
month	un mois	mí
moon	la lune	gealach
morning	le matin	maidin
mother	la mère	máthair
motor boat	une vedette	bád mótair
mountain	une montagne	sliabh
mouse	un souris	luch

kite
un cerf-volant
eitleog

mouth	la bouche	béal
mummy	maman	mamaí
mushroom	un champignon	muisiriún
my	mon, ma, mes (mon oncle/ma tante/mes jouets)	mo
name	un nom	ainm
neck	le cou	muineál
nest	un nid	nead
nephew	le neveu	nia
newspaper	un journal	nuachtán
niece	la nièce	neacht
night	une nuit	oíche
nine	neuf	a naoi
nineteen	dix-neuf	a naoi déag
nose	le nez	srón
November	novembre	Samhain
number	un chiffre, un numéro	uimhir
October	octobre	Deireadh Fómhair
office	un bureau	oifig
one	un, une	a haon
onion	un oignon	oinniún
orange (colour)	orange	oráiste
oval	un ovale, ovale	ubhchruth
overcoat	un pardessus	cóta mór
packet	un paquet	paicéad
to paint	peindre	dathaigh
paintbrush	un pinceau	scuab péinteála
painting	une peinture	pictiúr
paper	le papier	páipéar
parking meter	un parcomètre	méadar páirceála
passenger	un voyageur, une voyageuse	paisinéir
path (garden)	une allée	cosán
pavement	un trottoir	cosán
pear	une poire	piorra
pedal	une pédale	troitheán
pen	un stylo	peann
pencil	un crayon	peann luaidhe
pencil-sharpener	un taille-crayon	bioróir

penguin	un pingouin	*piongain*
people	les gens	*daoine*
pet	un animal familier	*peata*
photograph	une photographie	*grianghraf*
piano	un piano	*pianó*
picture	un tableau	*pictiúr*
pig	un cochon	*muc*
pillow	un oreiller	*piliúr*
pink	rose	*bándearg*
plant	une plante	*planda*
plate	une assiette	*pláta*
platform	un quai	*ardán*
to play	jouer	*imir*
please	s'il te plaît, s'il vous plaît	*le do thoil*
plough	une charrue	*céachta*
policeman	un agent (de police)	*garda*
pond (garden)	un bassin	*lochán*
porter	un porteur	*póirtéir*
post office	un bureau de poste	*oifig an phoist*
potato	une pomme de terre	*práta*
present	un cadeau	*bronntanas*
to pull	tirer	*tarraing*
pupil (primary school)	un écolier, une écolière	*dalta (bunscoile)*
pupil (secondary school)	un élève, une élève	*dalta (meánscoile)*
puppy	un chiot	*coileán*
purple	violet, violette	*corcra*
to push	pousser	*brúigh*
pyjamas	un pyjama	*culaith leapa*
pyramid	une pyramide	*pirimid*
rabbit	un lapin	*coinín*
radio	une radio	*raidió*
raft	un radeau	*rafta*
railway line	la voie ferrée	*bóthar iarainn*
rain	la pluie	*báisteach*
rainbow	un arc-en-ciel	*bogha báistí*
raincoat	un imperméable	*cóta báistí*
raspberry	une framboise	*sú chraobh*
to read	lire	*léigh*
rectangle	un rectangle	*dronuilleog*
red	rouge	*dearg*
refreshment kiosk	un buffet	*siopa bia*
to ride (= to go horse riding)	faire de l'équitation	*dul ag marcaíocht*
right	la droite	*ar dheis*
river	une rivière, un fleuve	*abhainn*
road	la chaussée/une route	*bóthar*
rock	un rocher	*carraig*
rolling-pin	un rouleau	*crann fuinte*
roof	un toit	*díon*
rose	une rose	*rós*
rowing-boat	un bateau à rames	*bád rámhaíochta*
rubber	une gomme	*scriosán*
ruler	une règle	*rialóir*
to run	courir	*rith*
runway	une piste d'envol	*rúidbhealach*
saddle	une selle	*diallait*
sail	une voile	*seol*
sand	le sable	*gaineamh*
sandal	la sandale	*cuarán*
satchel	un cartable	*mála scoile*
Saturday	samedi	*Satharn*
saucer	une soucoupe	*sásar*
saucepan	une casserole	*sáspan*
scales (pair of)	une balance	*meá*
school	une école	*scoil*

scissors	les ciseaux	*siosúr*
sea	la mer	*farraige*
seagull	une mouette	*faoileán*
seaweed	le varech	*feamainn*
see-saw	une bascule	*maide corrach*
September	septembre	*Meán Fómhair*
seven	sept	*a seacht*
seventeen	dix-sept	*a seacht déag*
she	elle	*í/sí*
sheep	un mouton	*caora*
shelf	un rayon	*seilf*
shell	une coquille	*sliogán*
ship	un navire	*long*
shirt	une chemise	*léine*
shoes	les chaussures, les souliers	*bróga*
to shut	fermer	*dún*
to sing	chanter	*can*
singer	un chanteur, une chanteuse	*amhránaí*
sink (kitchen)	un évier	*doirteal*
sister	une soeur	*deirfiúr*
to sit (be seated)	être assis (be seated); s'asseoir (to sit down)	*suigh*
sitting-room	un salon	*seomra suite*
six	six	*a sé*
sixteen	seize	*a sé déag*
skip (with skipping rope)	sauter à la corde	*scipeáil*
skirt	une jupe	*sciorta*
sky	le ciel	*spéir*
to sleep	dormir; s'endormir (to go to sleep)	*dul a chodladh*
slipper	une pantoufle	*slipéar*
to smell (a flower etc)	sentir	*bolaigh*
to smile	sourire	*déan meangadh*
snow	la neige	*sneachta*
snowman	un bonhomme de neige	*fear sneachta*
soap	le savon	*gallúnach*
sock	la chaussette	*stoca*
sofa	un canapé	*tolg*
soft	doux, douce	*bog*
son	un fils	*mac*
spade	une bêche (garden); une pelle (seaside)	*spád*
to speak	parler	*labhair*
spoon	une cuillère	*spúnóg*
spring (season)	le printemps	*an t-earrach*
square	un carré	*cearnóg*
squirrel	un écureuil	*iora rua*
stairs	un escalier	*staighre*
stamp (postage)	un timbre-poste	*stampa*
to stand (= to be standing)	être debout, se tenir debout (to be standing); se lever (to get up)	*seas*
station	la gare	*stáisiún*
star	une étoile	*réalta*
stomach	l'estomac	*bolg*
stool	un tabouret	*stól*
to stop	s'arrêter	*stop*
stawberry	une fraise	*sú talún*
street	une rue	*sráid*
sugar	le sucre	*siúcra*
summer	l'été	*samhradh*
sun	le soleil	*grian*
Sunday	dimanche	*Domhnach*
supermarket	un supermarché	*ollmhargadh*
sweater	un chandail	*geansaí*
to swim	nager	*snámh*
swing	une balançoire	*luascán*

table	une table	bord
tail	une queue	eireaball
to take	prendre	tóg
to talk	parler	labhair
tap	un robinet	sconna
to taste	goûter	blais
taste (sense of)	le goût	blas
taxi	un taxi	tacsaí
to teach	enseigner	múin
teacher (primary school)	un instituteur, une institutrice	múinteoir
Teddy (-bear)	un nounours	teidí
telephone	un téléphone	teileafón
telephone box	une cabine téléphonique	bosca teileafóin
television set	un téléviseur	teilifíseán
ten	dix	a deich
tennis	le tennis	leadóg
tent	une tente	puball
there is, there are	il y a	tá
they	ils, elles	siad
thirteen	treize	a trí déag
three	trois	a trí
to throw	lancer, jeter	caith
thumb	le pouce	ordóg
Thursday	jeudi	Déardaoin
ticket	un ticket (bus, métro); un billet (railway, theatre)	ticéad
tie	une cravate	carbhat
time	l'heure	am
tired	fatigué, fatiguée	tuirseach
today	aujourd'hui	inniu
toe	le doigt de pied, l'orteil	barraicín
tomorrow	demain	amárach
tooth	la dent	fiacal
toothbrush	une brosse à dents	scuab fiacal
touch (sense of)	le toucher	tadhall
towel	une serviette	tuáille
town	une ville	baile mór
tractor	un tracteur	tarracóir
traffic lights	les feux (de circulation)	soilsí tráchta
train	un train	traein
tree	un arbre	crann
triangle	un triangle	triantán
trolley (supermarket)	un chariot	tralaí
trowel	une houlette	lián
trousers	un pantalon	brístí
Tuesday	mardi	Máirt
turkey	un dindon, une dinde	turcaí
to turn	tourner	cas
twelve	douze	á dó dhéag
twenty	vingt	fiche
two	deux	a dó
typewriter	une machine à écrire	clóscríobhán
tyre	un pneu	bonn
umbrella (beach)	un parasol	scáth gréine
uncle	un oncle	uncail
underground station	une station de métro	stáisiún an fhobhealaigh
underpants	un slip	brístíní
vegetables	les légumes	glasraí
very	très	an-
vest (men's)	un maillot de corps	veist
village	un village	sráidbhaile
to wake (up)	se réveiller	dúisigh
to walk	marcher	siúil
to want	vouloir	teastaigh
wardrobe	une garde-robe	vardrús
washing machine	une machine à laver	meaisín níocháin
wastepaper-basket	une corbeille à papier	ciseán bruscair
water	l'eau	uisce
watering-can	un arrosoir	canna spréite
wave (sea)	une vague	tonn
wave	saluer	croith (lámh)
we	nous	sinn/muid
to wear	porter	caith
Wednesday	mercredi	Céadaoin
week	une semaine	seachtain
what . . ?/what are you eating?	qu'est-ce que . .?/qu'est-ce que tu manges?	céard/céard atá á ithe agat?
wheel	une roue	roth
wheelbarrow	une brouette	barra rotha
where?	où?	cén áit?
white	blanc, blanche	bán
wife	une femme	bean chéile
wind	le vent	gaoth
window	une fenêtre	fuinneog
wine	le vin	fíon
wing	une aile	sciathán
winter	l'hiver	geimhreadh
woman	une femme	bean
wood	un bois	coill
wool	la laine	olann
worm	un ver	péist
wristwatch	une montre	uaireadóir
to write	écrire	scríobh
yacht	un voilier	luamh
year	un an, une année	bliain
yellow	jaune	buí
yesterday	hier	inné
zoo	un jardin zoologique, un zoo	zú

I am writing a letter to Maria.
J'écris à Maria.
Tá litir á scríobh agam chuig Maria.

"Thank you for your letter."
"Je te remercie de ta lettre."
"Go raibh maith agat as ucht do litreach."

"How are you? I am very well."
"Comment vas-tu? Moi, je vais bien."
"Conas tá tú? Tá mé go han-mhaith."

"I have a new pet. It is a hamster called Otto."
"J'ai un nouveau petit animal. C'est un hamster qui s'appelle Otto."
"Tá peata nua agam. Hamstar is ea é darb ainm Otto."

"It is very quiet tonight."
"Ce soir, tout est tranquille."
"Tá an oíche an-chiúin."

"I am tired and sleepy."
"Moi, je suis fatigué, j'ai sommeil."
"Tá mé tuirseach agus tá fonn codlata orm."

"Goodnight for now."
"Bonne nuit"
"Oíche mhaith.